AV-8B
HARRIER
JUMP JETS

Are you ready to take it to the extreme?
Torque books thrust you into the action-packed
world of sports, vehicles, and adventure. These books
may include dirt, smoke, fire, and dangerous stunts.
WARNING: read at your own risk.

Library of Congress Cataloging-in-Publication Data

David, Jack, 1968-
  AV-8B Harrier jump jets / by Jack David.
      p. cm. — (Torque: military machines)
  Includes bibliographical references and index.
  Summary: "Amazing photography and engaging information explain the technologies and
capabilities of AV-8B Harrier Jump Jets. Intended for students in grades 3 through 7"—Provided
by publisher.
  ISBN-13: 978-1-60014-233-8 (hardcover : alk. paper)
  ISBN-10: 1-60014-233-8 (hardcover : alk. paper)
  1. Harrier (Jet fighter plane)—Juvenile literature. I. Title.

  UG1242.F5D3463 2008
  623.74'63—dc22   2008019862

This edition first published in 2009 by Bellwether Media.

The photographs in this book are reproduced through the courtesy of the United States Department of
Defense.

Printed in the United States of America.

CONTENTS

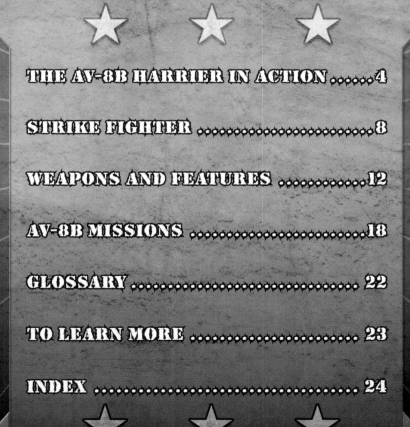

THE AV-8B HARRIER IN ACTION

A blast of heat hits the deck of an aircraft carrier as an AV-8B Harrier takes off. The plane's engine **nozzles** point down, pushing the plane straight up into the air. The Harrier hovers for a few seconds. Then it turns its nozzles and blasts forward.

A group of United States Marines is landing
on a nearby shore. An enemy helicopter is
flying to attack the Marines. The Harrier
shows up just in time. It launches a Sidewinder
missile. The missile streaks through the air and
smashes into the helicopter. An explosion fills
the sky. The Marines are safe. The Harrier's
mission is complete.

The militaries of Spain, Italy, and Great Britain also use the AV-8B.

STRIKE FIGHTER

The AV-8B Harrier is a strike fighter of the United States Marine Corps. It is the United States military's only **vertical/short takeoff and landing (V/STOL)** plane, or "jump jet." That means it can take off and land without a runway. It moves straight up and down like a helicopter. It also has the speed and power of a jet.

The U.S. Marine Corps has used several different versions of the Harrier since the plane entered service in 1985. The first version was the "Day Attack" Harrier. In 1991, the "Night Attack" Harrier, with special **radar**, entered service. Radar let pilots perform missions in the dark. The Harrier II Plus has even better radar, which allows it to launch guided missiles.

The U.S. Marine Corps used the AV-8B Harrier heavily in 1991's Operation Desert Storm. It flew 3,380 missions in the conflict.

WEAPONS AND FEATURES

The Harrier is loaded for battle. Its main gun is a GAU-12U Equalizer cannon. This 25-millimeter gun shoots big, powerful rounds.

13

The Harrier has seven **hardpoints** under the wings and the body. Missiles and bombs attach to these points. AIM-9 Sidewinders are air-to-air missiles. The Harrier can fire them at enemy aircraft. **Laser-guided bombs (LGBs)** and the AGM-65 Maverick missile are air-to-ground weapons mounted on the Harrier. The Harrier II Plus also carries the AIM-120 AMRAAM. This advanced missile uses radar to find targets.

AV-8B HARRIER SPECIFICATIONS:

Primary Function: Strike fighter

Length: 46 feet, 3 inches (14.1 meters)

Height: 11 feet, 7 inches (3.5 meters)

Weight: 12,800 pounds (5,806 kilograms)

Wingspan: 30 feet, 3 inches (9.2 meters)

Speed: 630 miles (1,014 kilometers) per hour

Range: 1,700 miles (2,736 kilometers)

★ FAST FACT ★

The AV-8B Harrier sometimes carries an anti-tank missile called the AGM-65 Maverick. It is built to blast through thick tank armor.

AV-8B MISSIONS

The AV-8B is a strike aircraft. Its main purpose is to destroy enemy targets in the air and on the ground. One of its most important jobs is to provide **close air support**. This means that it protects Marines on the ground. The Harrier can also fly patrols, **escort** other aircraft, and fly **reconnaissance** missions.

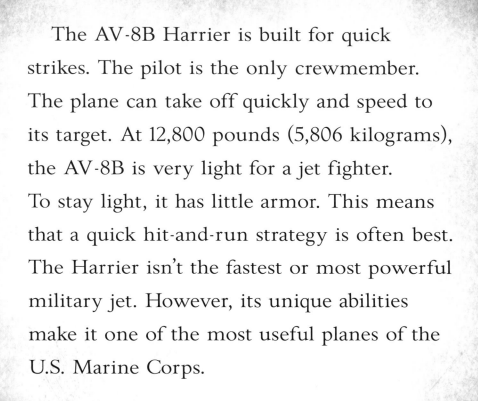

The AV-8B Harrier is built for quick strikes. The pilot is the only crewmember. The plane can take off quickly and speed to its target. At 12,800 pounds (5,806 kilograms), the AV-8B is very light for a jet fighter. To stay light, it has little armor. This means that a quick hit-and-run strategy is often best. The Harrier isn't the fastest or most powerful military jet. However, its unique abilities make it one of the most useful planes of the U.S. Marine Corps.

GLOSSARY

close air support—the role of supporting and protecting ground troops against enemy forces; close air support is a common mission of the AV-8B Harrier.

escort—to travel alongside and protect

hardpoint—a connection on a plane to which weapons or other equipment can be attached

laser-guided bomb (LGB)—an explosive that locks onto a target that has been marked with a laser

missile—an explosive launched at targets on the ground or in the air

mission—a military task

nozzle—the part of a jet engine from which superheated air is ejected, providing thrust

radar—a sensor system that uses radio waves to locate objects

reconnaissance—secret observation

vertical/short takeoff and landing (V/STOL)—the ability to takeoff and land without a runway

TO LEARN MORE

AT THE LIBRARY

Beyer, Julie. *Jet Fighter: The Harrier AV-8B*. New York: Children's Press, 2000.

David, Jack. *United States Marine Corps*. Minneapolis, Minn.: Bellwether, 2008.

Hansen, Ole Steen. *The AV-8B Harrier Jump Jet*. Mankato, Minn.: Capstone, 2006.

ON THE WEB

Learning more about military machines is as easy as 1, 2, 3.

1. Go to www.factsurfer.com

2. Enter "military machines" into search box.

3. Click the "Surf" button and you will see a list of related web sites.

With factsurfer.com, finding more information is just a click away.

INDEX